Creative Calligraphy

Peter Halliday

KING*f*ISHER

NEW YORK

To Deanna, Alex, Jamie, and Lizzie
and not forgetting Shelley (for
sitting on the work).

KINGFISHER
Larousse Kingfisher Chambers Inc.
95 Madison Avenue
New York, New York 10016

First published in 1995
2 4 6 8 10 9 7 5 3
2 (TR) / 1299 / SC / HBM (FR) / 128JAMA

Text copyright © Kingfisher Publications Plc 1990
Illustrations copyright © Peter Halliday 1990

LIBRARY OF CONGRESS CATALOGING-IN-PUBLICATION DATA
Halliday, Peter
Creative Calligraphy / Peter Halliday – 1st American ed.
p. cm.
Includes Index.
1. Calligraphy – Juvenile literature. [1. Calligraphy.]
I. Title.
743.H18 1995
745.6 1 – dc20

ISBN 1-85697-539-8

Edited by Annabel Warburg
Designed by Robert Wheeler
Illustrations by Peter Halliday
Cover design by John Jameson

Photographic Acknowledgments

The publishers wish to thank the following for kindly
supplying photographs for this book:
Page 4 John Walmsley (*top*) The Hutchinson Library
(*bottom*); 5 Donald Jackson; 9 British Museum; 14 London
Transport Museum; 15 Victoria & Albert Museum; 18 Jenni
Grey and Designer Bookbinders; 22 Visual Arts Library;
26 British Library (*left*) Donald Jackson (*right*); 33 Visual Arts
Library; 37 Bennett, Lovatt & Associates Ltd; 38 British
Museum (*left*) Peter Clayton (*right*); 39 Visual Arts Library
(*left*) British Museum (*right*).

Picture Research: Elaine Willis

Author's acknowledgments:
Adrian George, Michael Gullick, Donald Jackson,
Jen Lindsay, Brody Neuenschwander (illustration on
page 21), Bennett, Lovett & Associates Ltd.

Printed in Hong Kong

CONTENTS

HOW DO WE USE LETTERING?

How many different kinds of letters did you notice last you time you rode through town? Next time, try counting them and notice how different they look. We see lettering all around us, giving us information, advertising the names of people and things, and giving us instructions.

Signwriters paint signs using many different kinds of letters. Printers use different letters, called **typefaces**, for books, magazines, and newspapers. Designers in advertising look for letters that will be bold and striking. We use handwriting to write letters to each other, and our writing is probably quite different when we put our names on books and folders.

▲ A signwriter painting letters with a brush and resting his hand on a *maulstick* so that he doesn t smudge his work. Notice that he is holding his paint in his left hand.

▼ Many different styles of lettering have been used to attract attention to each of these newspapers.

Pick up a magazine or newspaper and play "Spot the Difference." Choose a letter, perhaps your own initial, and find as many different versions as you can. Then work out what the differences are.

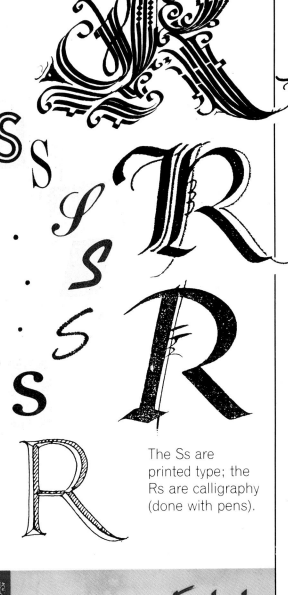

The Ss are printed type; the Rs are calligraphy (done with pens).

Calligraphy looks like particularly attractive handwriting, written very carefully. It is usually done using a pen or brush. Special documents, such as certificates and scrolls, may be written by a calligrapher. Calligraphers also design lettering for a printer to use or for a signwriter to copy. Calligraphers can make letters work in lots of different ways, to suit the subject and the purpose of what they are writing.

▶ Part of a scroll, called Royal Letters Patent, done by Donald Jackson, who is a scribe to the British Crown Office in the House of Lords. He made this in 1988 using gold paint and ink. It is a hand-made copy of the original.

5

LETTERS AND PATTERNS

Letters make patterns make words.
To begin calligraphy you will need to practice writing patterns so that your letters are even. Letters are pattern shapes. When we put these shapes together we can make words—our patterns then have meanings.

Try copying these patterns with a pencil or a fine felt-tipped pen. Make them as even as you can and try not to stop. If you do have to stop, lift your pencil or pen off of the paper and then carefully start over where you left off.

The arrows show the directions of the pen strokes.

(See page 37 for tips on holding pens if you are left-handed.)

When you can make really even patterns, try making patterns out of letters shaped like these below. You will notice that the patterns that you were making earlier are hidden inside the letter shapes.

6

With plenty of practice, you will find that you are able to make designs and pictures like the ones shown here. Copy the easy ones first, and then try the bigger, more complicated ones. You will then be good enough to make up your own designs.

Hold your pen or pencil comfortably—don't grip it tightly—and make sure that you can see the tip without having to move your head to one side.

Some pens are made especially for calligraphy and have chisel-shaped tips like this . . . .

HOLD THE PEN IN ONE POSITION FOR THIS

With tips like this you can make thick and thin strokes and make the patterns more varied. You can see right away that pens like these give the letters more character. They make the spaces inside the letters more interesting too, so that they show through.

·U·S·E· GUIDE·LINES·TO·HELP·/·/·/·/·/·/·

7

"MAKE YOUR OWN CAPITALS"

ITALIC. Italic is a streamlined version of the Small Roman hand (see pages 14–15), and it was developed for use in the Italian chancery or legal offices at the same time that the Small Roman was becoming popular in Italy. It is sometimes called "Chancery hand." Modern italic type is similar to italic writing. "Copperplate" handwriting is a later and modified form of italic from which our modern handwriting has developed.

ABCDEFGHIJKLMN

abcdefghijklmnopqrstuvwxyz

"CAPITALS ARE NO HIGHER THAN ASCENDERS"

ABCDEFGHIJ

&   AMPERSAND = FROM LATIN ET = AND   & &

x-height is about 5 nib widths

ascender

descender

START

FINISH

The Baite by John Donne

► A poem by John Donne, written using italic calligraphy in ink and decorated using real fishing flies, paint, and *Plexiglas* by Peter Halliday in 1982.

8

Italic narrow sloping & flowing

Italic LETTERS ARE SQUEEZED NARROW

1234567890!?.;'"

=NUMBERS CAN ASCEND & DESCEND= 1234567890"

KLMNOPQRSTUVWXYZ

=PEN ANGLE=
Your pen must always make the thin stroke in the same direction

only flourish where there is room

► A page from a volume presented to Henry VIII of England. It was written in the italic style in Italy in 1520.

PANDVLPHI
COLLENVCII PISAVRENSIS
APOLOGVS·
CVI TITVLVS
AGENORIA

OPQRSTUVWXYZ
st hy e po

MOBILES AND DECORATIONS

You can make mobiles to hang from the ceiling or from shelves. The first mobiles that you make could just hang straight down, but you will probably soon want to be more adventurous and make mobiles like the one shown below.

MOBILES

You will need: shapes made out of stiff paper or thin cardboard; pens; a needle; thread; thin sticks or bits of twig or wire.

1. Decorate the paper shapes using patterns like the ones on pages six and seven.

2. Using the needle, make a hole at the top of each shape, and use the thread to tie one shape to each end of a stick or piece of wire.

3. Find the point where the stick hangs level, and tie a thread around the stick at this point. Tie the other end of the thread to one end of a second stick.

4. Tie a shape to the other end of the second twig so that it balances. Then keep adding more layers, adjusting the balance as the mobile gets bigger.

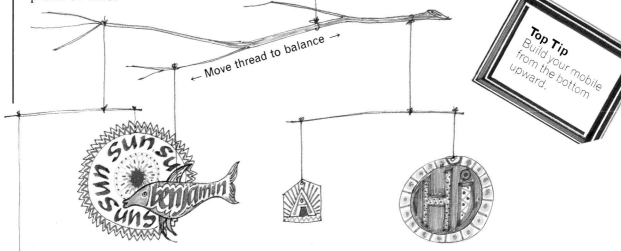

← Move thread to balance →

Top Tip
Build your mobile from the bottom upward.

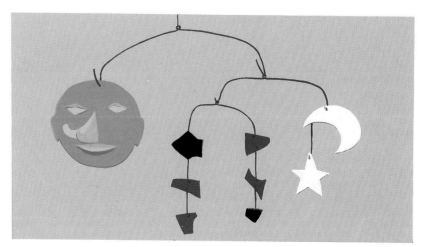

▶ Alexander Calder (1898 –1976) was an American artist who made mobiles like this one.

TABLE DECORATIONS

You can write on almost any object that has a smooth surface. Some surfaces will be better if they are painted matte-white first; otherwise the ink from your pen may not show up properly. Find an everyday saying or a name, and write it with a felt-tipped pen in such a way that it makes an interesting design. You could fill in the spaces with patterns. Here are some ideas to try:

Look for smooth, roundish pebbles. Lightly draw your design in pencil first. Then work with felt-tipped pens or paints.

Make a tag or pendant out of a piece of wood. Ask an adult to drill a hole through the top.

Thread through

Use two pieces of thin cardboard 6 x 3½ inches. Fold one piece and draw letters. Cut out and draw around it on the other piece. Cut out. Glue down back of fold. Decorate, thread, and then hang up.

You can make standing decorations using thin cardboard, glue, and felt-tipped pens. Cut out and fold the cardboard as shown, then glue it twice onto a base made from thick cardboard.

Make your own wrapping paper to wrap up presents or to cover boxes or desk organizers. Use a large sheet of plain paper, and decorate it with a design that you can repeat, using pens, crayons, or pencils.

COLLAGES

As we have already seen, letters can be arranged as interlocking shapes. An attractive and decorative way of putting lots of letters together is to make a collage. You could also make a "stained glass window" to hang up in your window.

A COLLAGE OF ONE LETTER

You will need: scissors, glue, magazines and newspapers, paper to glue the collage onto, pencils, felt-tipped pens.

We saw on page seven that there are lots of different styles and shapes of the same letter. Find some that are big enough to cut out easily (at least half an inch in height). See how many different styles of the same letter you can find.

Look at the shapes at the endings of the letter strokes (called *serifs*): the differences in thickness and whether or not they slope.

To make a collage out of the letters, arrange them in the shape of the letter they represent and glue them down.

MORE COLLAGES

You can make attractive collages using lots of differing styles to spell out names. Always make sure that your design fits comfortably onto your paper before you start gluing it down.

MAKE A STAINED GLASS WINDOW

Here are two ways of making a collage into a stained glass window. When you hold it up, the light will shine through the tissue or tracing paper.

Charlie

Contrast the lettering, and make some lively and amusing labels.

You will need: sheets of black construction paper, tracing paper, colored marker pens for **A**, colored tissue paper for **B**, glue, a black felt-tipped pen or marker pen, a small pointed pair of scissors.

WINDOW A

1. Cut a hole in a piece of black paper.
2. Cut a piece of tracing paper that is smaller than the black paper but big enough to cover the hole. Glue the two pieces of paper together.
3. Design a collage that will fit into the hole; draw it on another sheet of black paper. Cut out the design and glue it onto the tracing paper.
4. To make your collage look like pieces of stained glass, draw in some lines on the tracing paper using a black pen. Color in the pieces of "glass."

WINDOW B

1. Draw a design on a piece of black paper, leaving a margin of about 3/4 inch all the way around your design. Make sure that all the details in the design touch either another detail or the outer margin.
2. Carefully cut out the spaces in between the details in the design.
3. On the back of the design, glue pieces of colored tissue paper across the spaces you have cut out.
4 Draw any extra details you want on the tissue paper, using a black pen.

A

B

13

SMALL ROMAN OR BOOKHAND. In the 1300s, scholars in Italy, called "Humanists," copied this lettering from books written in the 700s. The style is often called "Humanistic" and some of the early printed books from 15th-century Italy used styles copied from it. Small Roman soon became the standard Roman type that we still use today. The capitals are based on the ones used during the time of the Roman Empire (27 B.C.–A.D. 476). (This caption is printed using "Palatino" a typeface designed this century by Hermann Zapf using models from early Italian printers.)

abcdefghijklmnopqrstuv

LOOK AT THE SIZE OF THE COUNTER TO WORK OUT HOW LARGE TO WRITE #

◀ The London Underground (subway) map lettering designed by Edward Johnston in 1916, was based on his studies of Carolingian and Humanistic calligraphy.

Journey planner

ABCDEFGHIJKLMNO

New York

London ~ Paris

Lucie ~ Alice

Benjamin

14

ROMAN LETTER
1st Century AD

▶ A page from a book, written and decorated in Italy around 1500, in the Humanistic style. Notice the Roman capitals, both written and painted, and the clear simplicity of the writing. The book is called the Bentivoglio Hours.

wxyz 1234567890?!;:

O ns

THE SMALL LETTERS ARE ROUND IN SHAPE "
THE COUNTERS ARG OPEN

KEEP PEN AT
THIS ANGLE

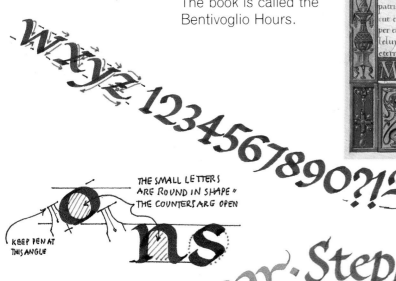

Caspar · Stephanie

PQRSTUVWXYZ

MAKE THE CAPITALS
QUITE SMALL

&

& & &

Ampersands

Charlie Chaplin

MAKE YOUR OWN BOOK

Making your own book is not as difficult as you might imagine. A book is only a number of sheets of paper joined together in order.
Here are some ideas for making simple books.

MAKING A ZIGZAG BOOK

You will need: a piece of plain paper (8½ by 11 inches); pencil; ruler; scissors; glue; pens; thin cardboard.

1. Fold the plain paper lengthwise, and cut it in half.

2. Fold each half of paper into a zigzag of four. Join the two zigzags together by gluing a narrow strip at the back of two edges. You will then have a zigzag book that has eight sides.

3. Fold the zigzag together. Make a cover by gluing some thin cardboard on each end.

Each page should have a similar layout.

◀ You can decorate the margins.

Margin

▲ Leave a margin all the way around each page, as shown above. The lower margin should be wider than the others. The space inside the margins is called the text area. Put all your writing and design inside this area.

4. When you have decided on the subject matter, put your designs on the pages.

Some ideas for subject matter:
– put one letter of your name on each page, and use some of your patterns from pages six and seven as a frame
– find a poem and fit a verse onto each page
– put a picture on the left-hand page and some writing on the page opposite

Top Tip
Use small amounts of glue, and wait for it to stick.

Top Tip
Don't forget that you can use both sides of the book.

MAKE A SINGLE SECTION BOOK

6

The writing and illustrations in handmade books are usually all completed before the pages are sewn together, but here you can make the book first and then decide what to put into it.

You will need: three sheets of plain paper (8½ by 11 inches); one sheet of colored thin cardboard (11½ by 17 inches), folded in half for the cover; a piece of embroidery thread (or similar); a needle; a ruler; a pencil; pens; paints or crayons for decorating (optional).

1. Fold each sheet of paper in half across the width, and slip the sheets into each other; slip the paper into the folded cardboard that you have chosen for the cover.

▲ A hand-bound book, called a "fine binding." The flat box behind the book is a slipcase, used to protect the book. This fine binding was made by Jenni Grey.

Paper

Fold

Thin cardboard for cover

2. Keeping the pages and cover together, measure halfway down the inside fold (called the "gutter"), mark, and make a hole with a needle through all the sheets of paper and cardboard. Make sure the hole is exactly in the fold. Make two more marks in the gutter, one between the center and the top and one between the center and the bottom. Using the needle, make holes through these marks.

Slip each folded page inside the others

Top Tip
It is a good idea to make a "mock-up" book to try out your ideas.

3. Following the diagrams carefully, sew the thread through the gutter. Make sure that you start on the inside and take the thread through to the outside. Finish by sewing the thread through the hole where you started, back to the inside.

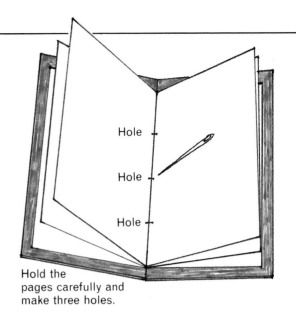

Hole

Hole

Hole

Hold the pages carefully and make three holes.

Sew the thread through the gutter.

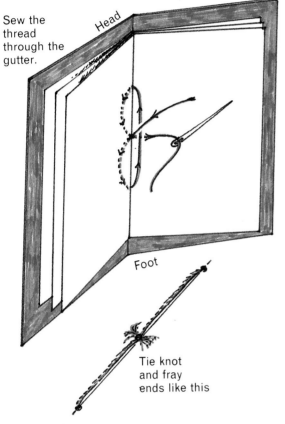

Head

Foot

Tie knot and fray ends like this

4. Tie a neat knot over the long thread that runs down the gutter. Cut the thread about half an inch from the knot, and fray the ends out with the point of the needle so that the knot cannot come undone.

5. Draw your ideas for designs on some practice paper. Follow the diagram below, showing the size of the margins and mark out guidelines lightly on each page. Put your design into the book.

Page plan

▲ If your text is short, use wider margins to center it on the page.

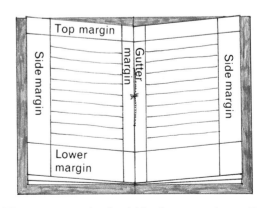

Top margin

Side margin

Gutter margin

Side margin

Lower margin

(The gutter margin should be the same size as the side margins but split on either side of the fold.)

6. If you want to make a longer book, you can add extra sheets of plain paper (8 1/2 by 11 inches) before you sew it together. Each sheet, folded, adds four more pages.

GOTHIC OR BLACK LETTER. This developed in the countries of northern Europe from about 1200 and was used until the 1500s, when books began to be printed rather than hand-written. The reason it is called "black letter" is that the heavy black letters are so closely spaced that the pages of writing look black. It is also called "Old English." The first printed book was printed in this style by Johann Gutenberg in Germany around 1450.

20

Gothic

or Black letter

▲ Part of a poem by John Donne, written in the gothic style by Brody Neuenschwander in 1989. This is his design version, done in ink on top of bronze powder paint.

BUILD UP PATTERNS BIT BY BIT

hijklmn uvwxyz

KEEP PEN ANGLE THE SAME ALWAYS

opqrstuvwxyz

MAKE THIN LINES BY TURNING ON ITS CORNER

IF YOU WANT TO WRITE LIKE THIS YOU MUST PRACTICE LIKE THIS

Calligraphy

SCROLL AND CASE

The earliest books were made by the ancient Egyptians almost 4,500 years ago. They were written on scrolls—long strips of a paper made from a reed called papyrus, which were stored rolled up around a stick. Even today, some documents and certificates are written on special paper or parchment and made into scrolls.

MAKING A SCROLL AND CASE

You will need: thin cardboard (8 ½ by 11 inches); a piece of ribbon about 10 inches long; a cardboard tube about 12 inches long; thin white cardboard measuring 2 ½ by 8 ½ inches; a pencil; a ruler; scissors; glue; pens; a strip of thin wood or thick cardboard 9 inches long; sandpaper; paper for covering the scroll case (optional).

▼ A scroll with the seal still attached. It was written for King Richard I of England in 1194. Being a legal document, it was folded at the bottom up to the last line of writing, and then ribbon was threaded through so that nothing could be added afterward without breaking the seal.

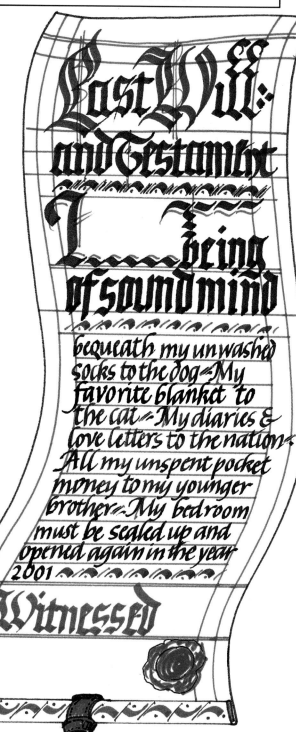

Last Will and Testament I .... being of sound mind .... bequeath my unwashed socks to the dog. My favorite blanket to the cat. My diaries & love letters to the nation. All my unspent pocket money to my younger brother. My bedroom must be sealed up and opened again in the year 2001. Witnessed

1. Design some showy flourishes for the top of the scroll, but do lots of practice first so that you can get them right.

2. Write out the message clearly and attractively, leaving a space of about 1 inch at the bottom of the scroll.

3. Fold the bottom of the scroll over the thin strip of wood or thick cardboard.

4. Tie the ribbon as shown in the illustration.

Fold paper over strip glue in place

Strip of wood or cardboard

Roll up and tie the ribbon

Hole

Make a hole and tie the ribbon through like this

5. To make the case, ask an adult to cut off about 3 inches of the cardboard tube. With fine sandpaper, smooth off the rough edges. Roll up the strip of thin cardboard and glue it into the top of the long tube, leaving about 1½ inches sticking up. The short piece of the tube will fit over the cardboard as a lid for your case.

You can decorate the case by covering it with wrapping paper. (See page 11 for instructions on how to make your own wrapping paper.)

Glue in place

Overlap and glue along edge.

Cover

Cut flaps and glue to cover end before covering sides

23

SIMPLE LAYOUTS

Making a design to go on such things as birthday cards, gift tags, and labels needs a little planning to make it fit properly and look as you would like. It is easiest if you first make a rough design, called a "layout." You can "lay out" your idea on paper in such a way that you can scribble over it to change and improve it.

You will need: practice paper; good-quality thin cardboard or stiff paper; pencil; pens; glue; scissors.

When you plan a design, you may find that part of it is all right but that you want to change the rest. Rather than re-doing the whole design, you can make your changes on another sheet of paper (be sure that the paper is the right size). You can then cut the new piece out and paste it in position on your original design.

When you are satisfied with the whole design (you can cut out and paste as much as you like), you will have what is called a "paste-up," which is a complete design that you can copy or trace.

Start with small rough sketches of the layout

When you have experimented with your rough layout until you are happy with it, you can copy your final design on cardboard or stiff paper.

Concertina fold cards

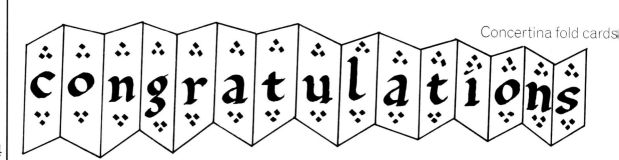

24

Don't be too disappointed if you can't get things right at first: you will get better with practice.

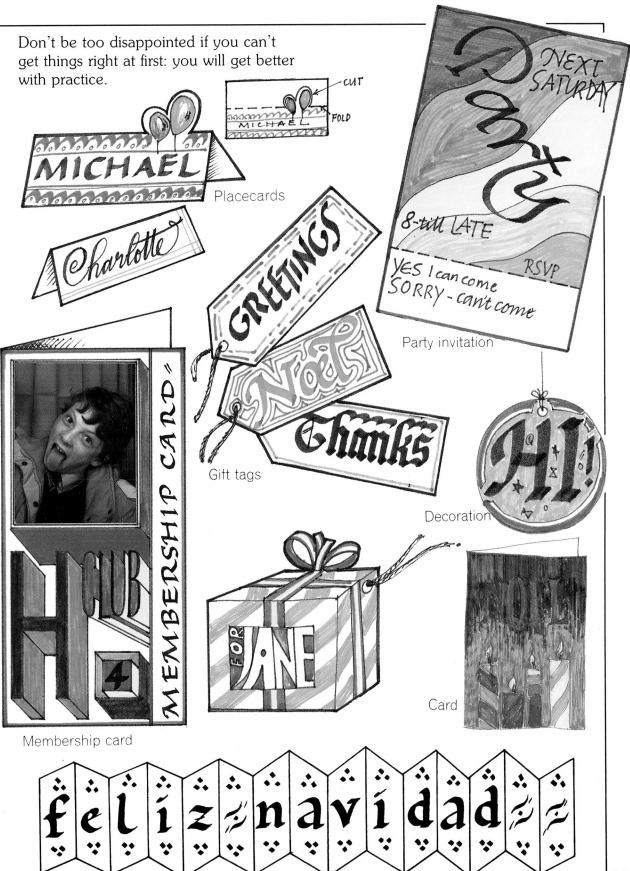

Placecards

Party invitation

Gift tags

Decoration

Membership card

Card

DECORATING INITIALS

A clever way of using letters is to decorate or "illuminate" them. There are lots of ways of decorating letters—look at signs and advertisements to get some good ideas.

You can start by making a design on some paper and coloring it in. Always make sure that the letter shape shows clearly. If you make the decoration too complicated, the letter will be difficult to recognize.

◀ In the days before books were printed, special books had initials that were highly decorated. They were often "illuminated" by the addition of shining gold leaf to the letter or background. This letter "H" is from a 12th-century manuscript.

▲ A page from a sampler of initials and heraldic devices painted and illuminated by Donald Jackson in 1988.

DRAW IN THE OUTLINE FIRST

MAKE A BUTTON BADGE

Make a button badge from thick cardboard. Stick a safety pin to the back with tape.

Build up multi-stroke letters bit by bit. Make sure that the gap in between is even.

DESIGNING MONOGRAMS

A monogram is a design linking together two or more letters (for example, your initials). A monogram can be used just for decoration, or for putting on stationery, or to put on stickers for labeling your things. Draw several ideas lightly in pencil first, to find the best one. It is a good idea to make the initials weave in and out of each other, or to join and merge letters.

Design your own coat of arms.

PLH

DESIGN USING 'S' AND 'O'

Versal letter P

Versals were originally used at the beginning of a verse or paragraph.

27

WORD PICTURES

We have already seen how to make patterns from letters and create words (pages six and seven). Words can also be made into patterns and pictures. These are called **calligrams.**

There are many ways of making calligrams. First, try some simple ideas like those shown here. Some are made from letters only, not words. You can make them by repeating the same words and fitting them into the shape representing the subject of the word. You can even write short descriptions or poems.

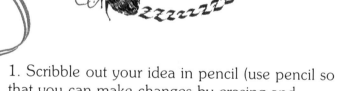

1. Scribble out your idea in pencil (use pencil so that you can make changes by erasing and working over).

2. When you have worked out your idea, draw just the outline, in pencil again, then start writing with the pen.

3. You may want to change the size of your pen or try out different colors.

Start with easy shapes like
these . . . when you find out
how easy it is you will want
to make more clever
calligrams.

alphabutterfly

spaghetti

GRAPHICS-1

Calligraphy and lettering can be attractive and decorative, but they can also be used to make many useful things. Why not impress your friends by making your own letterhead, membership card, or cassette insert?

MAKING A CASSETTE INSERT

You will need: Cassette case; cassette insert (to draw around); practice paper; thin cardboard or stiff paper; pencil; ruler; scissors; pens; glue.

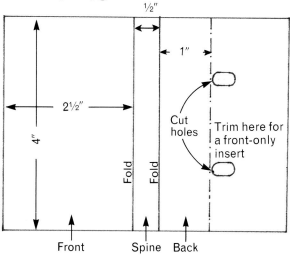

½"

1"

2½"

4"

Fold

Fold

Cut holes

Trim here for a front-only insert

Front   Spine   Back

1. Find a cassette insert and draw around it on the thin cardboard or stiff paper to make a shape to put your design on.

Try out some rough designs in color to get a good idea of how your cassette insert will look.

2. Try out three or four designs, in rough first, on the practice paper. Color them in roughly. Cut and fold them to size, and see what they look like in the case.

3. Select the best design and draw it on the paper carefully and lightly in pencil. Color in your design. This can be your final version or a final rough (sometimes called a visual). Fold it and put it into the cassette case.

Look at the ideas illustrated here, and decorate some
writing paper with your own letterhead.
Turn to pages 26 and 27 for some more
ideas for ways of decorating your initials.

Top Tip
You could try using
typeface letters
from your collage
designs on pages
12 and 13.

172 Main Street Anytown
Tel 123·456·789

HARRY ZEITGEIST

Top Tip
Use the cut and
paste techniques
described on
pages 22 and 23.

Invitation
COME TO THE CONCERT

Invitation   Invitation

If you have access to a photocopier, do
your designs in black or in pencil outline
so that you can do several copies, and
then color them in by hand.

GRAPHICS-2

Some of the most dramatic use of lettering has been on posters and in advertising. Often the designers combine lettering with pictures, but sometimes printers use lots of different type, which creates an amazing variety of patterns.

Making Dramatic Use of Letters

When making posters and advertisements, you need good ideas to get your message across, clear and well-chosen letter forms, and a well-organized design. Work out your idea in an order of priorities like this:

● What does your poster need to do?—(advertise a disco, dance, school play?).
● What is the most important part of your message? Work out an order of importance (e.g. what, when, where, how much, etc.).

● Think of a bold picture or pattern that is relevant to the event and will attract attention.

When designing a poster, start by making a few rough "thumbnail" sketches, then choose the best one to work on at full size. Follow the cut and paste techniques for the original layout, as described on pages 22 and 23.

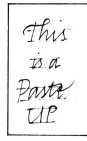

Start with thumbnail sketches.

This is a PASTE UP

Try out the lettering you have chosen.

Draw some rules and do some careful versions of the lettering.

Select the best letters and paste them down. Check the spacing between the letters and words.

◀ Designers of book jackets often try to use lettering to suit the subject of the book.

The technique used for designing posters can be used for anything in which visual impact is important: advertising, book jackets, or package design.

Designers often get inspiration from all kinds of different sources, so watch out for new ideas. You could start to keep a scrapbook of examples of lettering you find striking and interesting. It is also a good idea to keep a sketchbook, so that you can make small, rough sketches.

▲ Throughout the 20th century, artists and designers have used lettering and painting in creative ways in posters like this one by E. Heckel.

Perspective

Make all lines join at the vanishing point.

The farther away you put the vanishing point, the more you appear to be looking up (or down) at the word.

Vanishing point

Vanishing point

Lettering on a curve

Cut out each letter.

1. Draw the lettering in a straight line, and cut out each letter.
2. Using a compass, draw two lines as a guide. The distance between the lines should be the same as the height of the letters.
3. Lay down the letters, check the spacing, and paste in position.
4. Copy or trace for use on the final version.

Draw guidelines using a compass. The distance between them should be the height of the letters.

MAKING PENS

Have you noticed the number of different pens it is possible to buy? Next time you go to a stationery store, you will probably see lots: ballpoints, felt-tips, cartridge pens . . . . The prices vary greatly, too.

Until about 150 years ago, making a pen would have been something that all schoolchildren would have learned to do. The only pens available were **quills**, which were made from feathers. Being able to cut and sharpen a quill-pen with a penknife was a basic skill. Some calligraphers still use quills today, because they feel that they are better for certain special pieces of calligraphy.

With a fine pointed brush you can paint fine lines by just touching the paper with the tip, or you can thicken the stroke by pressing harder and you can move the brush sideways. Experiment and try out various paints and colors. The flat, one-stroke brushes can be used in the same way as a pen, but if you press a little harder the stroke will be thicker.

Quill pen
Quills must be treated to harden them and are best when cut by an expert using a quill knife.

Side view   Below

Almost anything that is strong enough and is shaped like a narrow tube can be made into a pen. The important thing is the shape of the nib. Ask an adult to help you cut the end of the tube into the shape illustrated here for the reed pen (*below*). To write with your pen, dip the nib into fountain pen ink.

Reed pen
Must be cut with a sharp knife to this shape (ask an adult to help).

Below
Side view

Fine pointed brush (sable or imitation sable).

Flat "one-stroke" brush

TRY THIS

Tie two pencils or two felt-tipped pens together and make "double" letters and patterns.

MAKING YOUR OWN FELT PEN

You will need: a spring clip; Styrofoam; thin felt or a piece of old blanket or a piece of quilting (such as that used for parkas); scissors.

Spring clip

Ink

Quilting or felt

1¼"

Styrofoam

1. Cut a piece of Styrofoam to the width of the clip and about 1¼ inches in depth.

2. Cut a piece of felt, blanket, or quilting to the same width as the Styrofoam and about 2¾ inches in depth.

3. Cover the Styrofoam with the felt or quilting and put them together into the clip, making sure that the covering is pulled tight.

The pen can be dipped into fountain pen ink and can be used on lining paper (used under wallpaper) or on large pieces of drawing paper. Although these pens are for quite large writing, you will find them fun to play around with and useful for posters. Be careful to put plenty of newspaper underneath.

FABRIC PAINTS AND DYES

Some crayons and felt-tipped pens and paints are specially made for drawing on fabrics. Use them to decorate T-shirts or scarves. You can either draw directly on the fabric or cut some templates and stencils first. Plan your design before you start—you can't make corrections! If you want to work on a T-shirt, put some stiff cardboard inside (to protect the back), and tape it to a flat board. Outline your design with soft pencil, and make sure that you follow the instructions for using the paints properly. Hold the area where you are working quite tightly, because fabric stretches when you work on it.

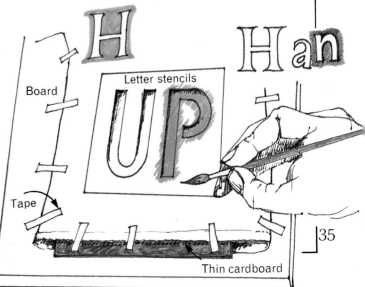

Board

Letter stencils

Tape

Thin cardboard

PENS, PAPERS, INKS, PAINTS

The information here is only a rough guide to the many different kinds of pens and supplies available. You may find a number of other types of pen. Try them out before you buy, so that you make sure you get what you want.

BEROL COLOR PEN
12 colors.

BEROL ITALIC PEN
4 sizes—5 colors.

REXEL CALLIGRAPHY PEN
Different sizes and colors.

FINE LINE Several colors.
Many different makes.

REXEL "WILLIAM MITCHELL" ROUND HAND PENS 10 pen sizes (dip pen). Left-handed version available.

PENS

Felt-tipped and fiber tip pens
cannot be refilled. Choose ones that are waterproof. **Cartridge pens** can be refilled by replacing the empty cartridge with a full one. Some are supplied with a refillable cartridge that can be filled with colored ink. Never use waterproof ink in a cartridge pen, and wash it thoroughly after changing the color. To use a **dip pen**, use ink in bottles, preferably non-waterproof. Dip just the tip into the ink. Have a paint rag or a paper towel handy to wipe the pen. Always wash the pen after use.

PAPERS

Most art stores will have a selection of pads and papers. Smooth writing paper or smooth drawing paper is suitable for calligraphy. Layout pads are useful because the paper is thin, so that you can see through it to work over designs in order to copy or change them. The paper also takes ink and color well. Colored "cover" papers can be used, and they will take ink or colors.

INKS AND PAINTS

The best kind of ink for calligraphy is one that is non-waterproof. Any ink for use in cartridge pens will be good for practice, but for best results get some calligraphy ink. The finest black inks are Chinese or Japanese inks, which often come in the form of short sticks and have to be ground with water. They can also be bought in liquid form. For

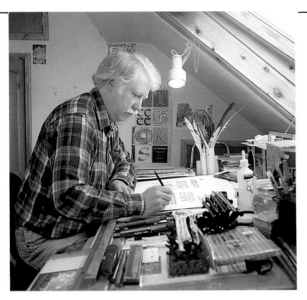

▲ The author at work.

drawing and outlining, use either a fineline felt-tipped pen or waterproof drawing ink.

Your local art store will have many different kinds of paints. Use watercolors, either in tubes, such as designer's gouache, or in small pans, as in painting sets.

IF YOU ARE LEFT-HANDED, follow the illustration below as a guide to holding your calligraphy and italic pens to make the thick and thin strokes at the proper angle. Turn your paper at an angle; move the paper slightly to the left and turn your wrist so that the edge of the pen makes the thin stroke at an angle of 45° to the line.

Position yourself and your work so that you can see what you have written. It helps to use a board which you can lean on at a slope against the work table.

PLATIGNUM CALLIGRAPHY/LETTERING CARTRIDGE PEN 3 nib sizes. Left-handed version available.

BRAUSE PENS Several different sizes (dip pen).

"AUTOMATIC" PEN for large work. Several sizes and shapes (dip pen).

COIT PEN for large work. Several sizes and shapes (dip pen).

OSMIROID CARTRIDGE PEN More than 30 nib sizes. Left-handed version available.

ROTRING ART PEN Cartridge pen. 3 sizes. (Can be used with Rotring Art Color.)

SHAEFFER CARTRIDGE PEN 3 nib sizes.

HISTORY OF WRITING

The way that we use calligraphy, lettering, and printing today is the result of many centuries of change. All writing and lettering came originally from the use of pictures to record information. We can still see examples of how prehistoric people painted pictures on cave walls to describe their hunting.

The most famous kind of picture writing is Egyptian hieroglyphic, meaning "sacred carved inscription," which was first used about 5,000 years ago. The idea of writing spread through different civilizations in the eastern Mediterranean. As the pictures were adapted for different languages or written using different tools, they became more streamlined and eventually changed into letters.

m	f	p	b	w	vowel sound does not exist in English	i
z or s	s	ch or sh	ch	h	h	r
dj	d	th	t	g	k	q

Hieroglyphs and their approximate sound

An Egyptian scribe

▲ The most important difference between hieroglyphs and earlier writing is that each picture represents a *sound*.

◀ Many Roman tablets and inscriptions survive today. We think that the letters were first painted with a flat brush and then "incised" by carving with a chisel to preserve them.

The Greeks were the first to use letters that we recognize today. They passed their letters on to the Romans, who developed the alphabet that we are familiar with today. They used only capital letters.

▼ Modern lettering artists still study Roman inscriptions today to improve their understanding of letters.

Sometimes they were filled with lead or bronze.

Cuneiform c.4000 B.C.

Stylus marks

Egyptian hieroglyphics 3100 B.C.–A.D. 400

Phoenician c.700 B.C.

Classical Greek 500 B.C.

Writing on a soft clay tablet using a stylus.

Parchment (specially treated animal skin) gradually replaced earlier writing surfaces, such as papyrus and clay tablets. By A.D. 100, people had developed a method of folding sheets of parchment-papyrus and sewing them together to make a book. During the late 700s, the scholar Alcuin of York developed a style of writing that made books easier to plan and to read. Capitals were used for headings, and small letters, or "half uncials" were used for the main text. Books were made by hand until about 1500.

▲ Here a scribe is teaching his pupil. He has a special chair with a board fixed to it; the inkwell is placed in a hole on the board. He writes with a quill pen and is holding the parchment down with the tip of his penknife (used to sharpen his pen).

In around 1450 a German named Johann Gutenberg invented a method of printing using separate pieces of metal for each letter that could be arranged in any combination. This made it possible to produce many copies of the same book, and the metal, or type, could be used again. Until the early years of the 20th century, printing methods changed very little, although the machinery used became much more advanced. Since the 1950s, the development of *offset litho printing* and advances in micro-computers have revolutionized printing methods.

◀ A page from a book printed by the Venetian Aldus Manutius in 1499. He produced beautiful books in small and inexpensive volumes.

▶ A book printed by the Bauhaus—an influential school of design, founded in Germany in 1919.

Calligraphy *Calligraphy*
Calligraphy

▲ The most modern way of printing is to use a laser printer. This will print quickly and accurately and in any shape or style you choose.

| Roman B.C.–A.D. 300 | European A.D. 500–700 | Carolingian A.D. 780 | English A.D. 1000 | Gothic A.D.1200 | 17thC | 18thC | 20thC |

INDEX